AMAZING SCIENCE

PULL, LIFT, AND LOWER

A Book About Pulleys

by Michael Dahl
illustrated by Denise Shea

PICTURE WINDOW BOOKS
Minneapolis, Minnesota

Special thanks to our advisers for their expertise:

Youwen Xu, Professor
Department of Physics and Astronomy
Minnesota State University, Mankato, Minn.

Susan Kesselring, M.A.
Literacy Educator
Rosemount–Apple Valley–Eagan (Minnesota) School District

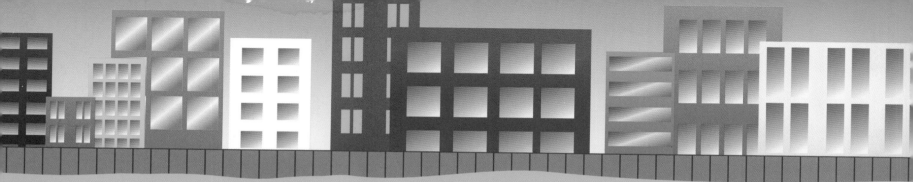

Editor: Jacqueline Wolfe
Designer: Joseph Anderson
Page Production: Joseph Anderson
Creative Director: Keith Griffin
Editorial Director: Carol Jones
The illustrations in this book were created digitally.

Picture Window Books
5115 Excelsior Boulevard
Suite 232
Minneapolis, MN 55416
877-845-8392
www.picturewindowbooks.com

Printed in the United States of America.

Library of Congress Cataloging-in-Publication Data
Dahl, Michael.
Pull, lift, and lower : a book about pulleys / by Michael Dahl ; illustrated by Denise Shea.
p. cm. — (Amazing science)
Includes bibliographical references and index.
ISBN 1-4048-1305-5 (hard cover)
1. Pulleys—Juvenile literature. I. Shea, Denise. II. Title. III. Series.
TJ147.D3235 2005
621.8'11—dc22
2005024975

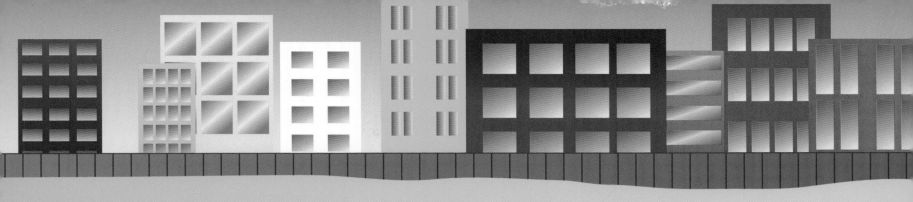

TABLE OF CONTENTS

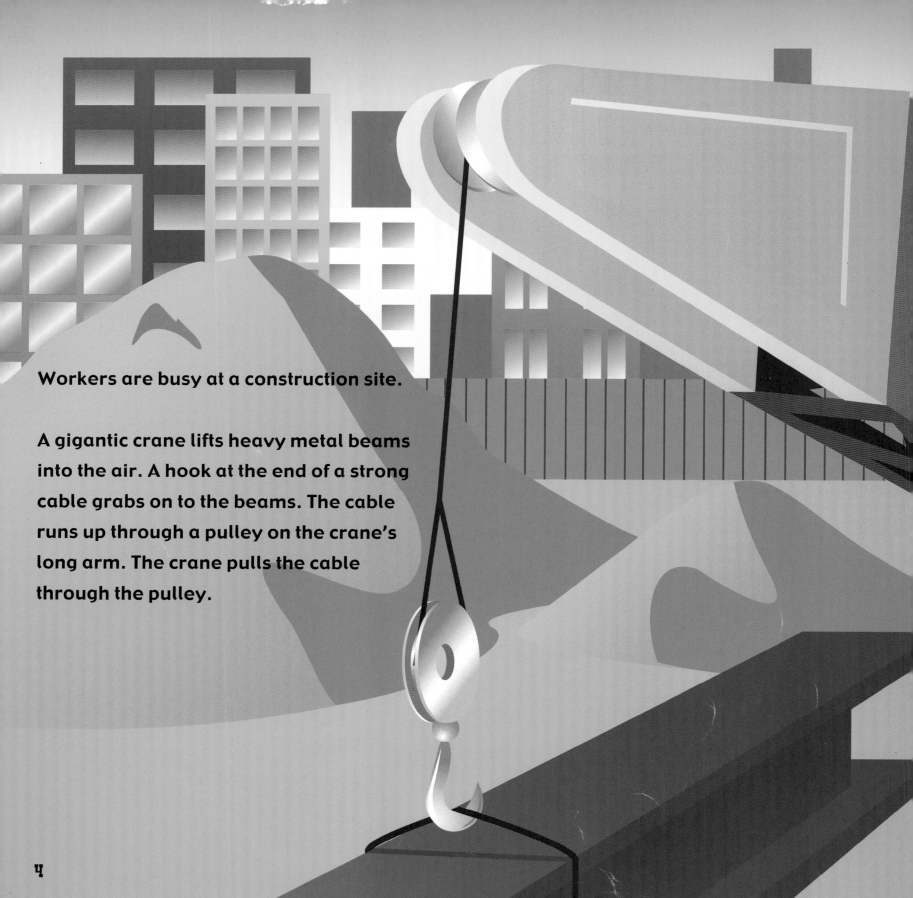

Workers are busy at a construction site.

A gigantic crane lifts heavy metal beams into the air. A hook at the end of a strong cable grabs on to the beams. The cable runs up through a pulley on the crane's long arm. The crane pulls the cable through the pulley.

A PULLEY IS A MACHINE

A pulley is a simple machine. A simple machine is anything that helps people do work. Work can mean lifting heavy loads or moving things up and down.

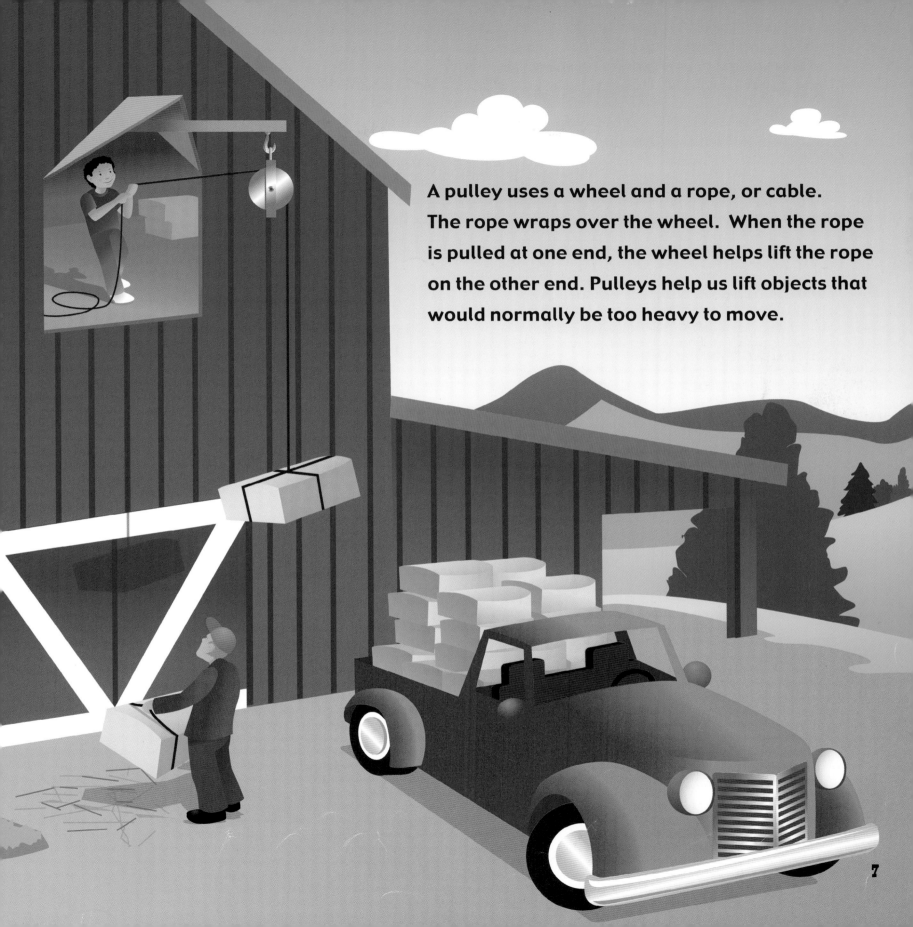

A pulley uses a wheel and a rope, or cable. The rope wraps over the wheel. When the rope is pulled at one end, the wheel helps lift the rope on the other end. Pulleys help us lift objects that would normally be too heavy to move.

WINDOW BLINDS

Open the window blinds. Pull down on the cord and the blinds rise, letting sunlight into the room. If you release, or lift up, the cord, the blinds lower back down.

Window blinds use a pulley. The cord wraps around a small wheel at the top. The tiny pulley can help lift or lower the blinds into place.

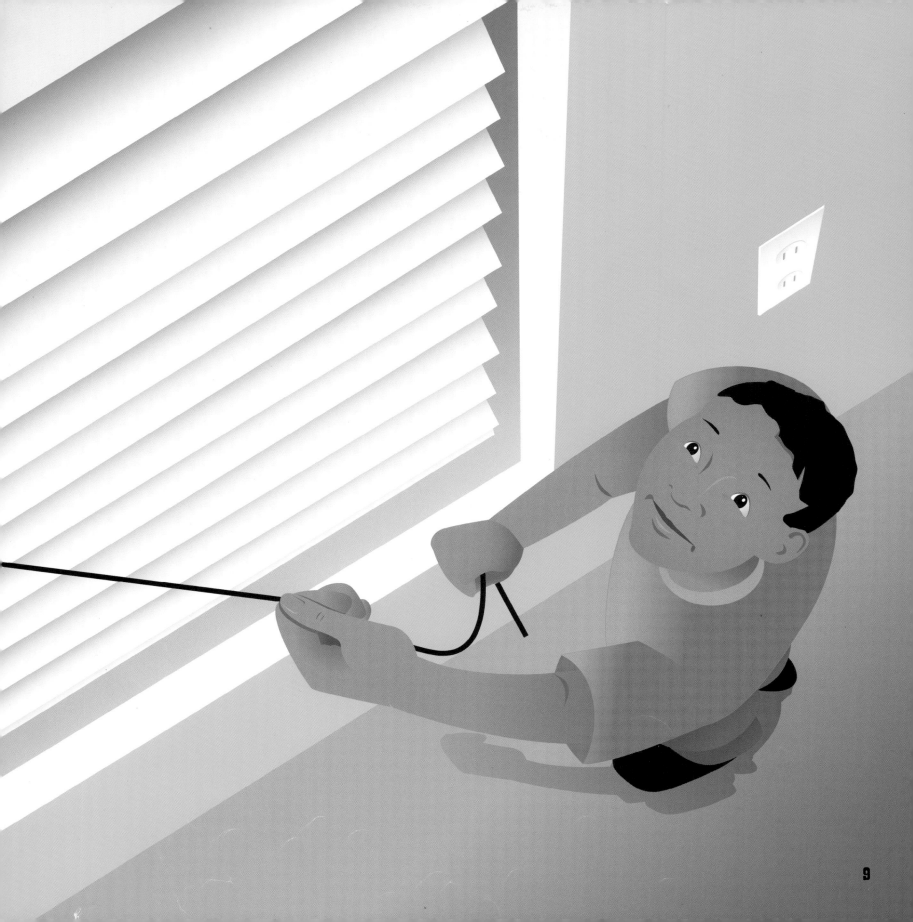

9

FLAGPOLES

Outside the school building, a flag is attached to a long rope. When one end of the rope is pulled down, the other end lifts the flag to the top of the tall pole. The flagpole uses a pulley to raise the flag to the top, where it flutters and flaps in the wind.

BLOCK AND TACKLE

Some pulleys use more than one wheel. More wheels make a load easier to lift. A block and tackle is a combination of several wheels and ropes that work together.

MOVING HEAVY SAILS

Block and tackle is used to hoist, or lift, heavy sails on a sailboat. The ropes that lift and lower sails are called halyards. Using a block and tackle, one person can lift a sail that weighs twice as much as a grown adult.

ELEVATORS

Step inside an elevator and push a button. Swoosh! The elevator car moves you smoothly up or down the elevator shaft.

Powerful metal pulleys lift and lower the elevator cars. When you push a button, a hidden motor pulls on a steel cable attached to the elevator car. The cables and wheels of the pulleys help you reach your floor.

FIRST-CLASS PULLEY

A first-class pulley uses a wheel that stays in one place. The pulley's rope moves up and down, and the wheel turns around a point called the axle. The axle on a first-class pulley never moves. It helps keep the wheel steady.

A first-class pulley helps people pull a bucket of water up a deep well. People all over the world use this type of pulley.

Up, up, up rise the heavy metal beams. The powerful crane uses its pulley to move large equipment and supplies.

Pulleys help the world keep moving.

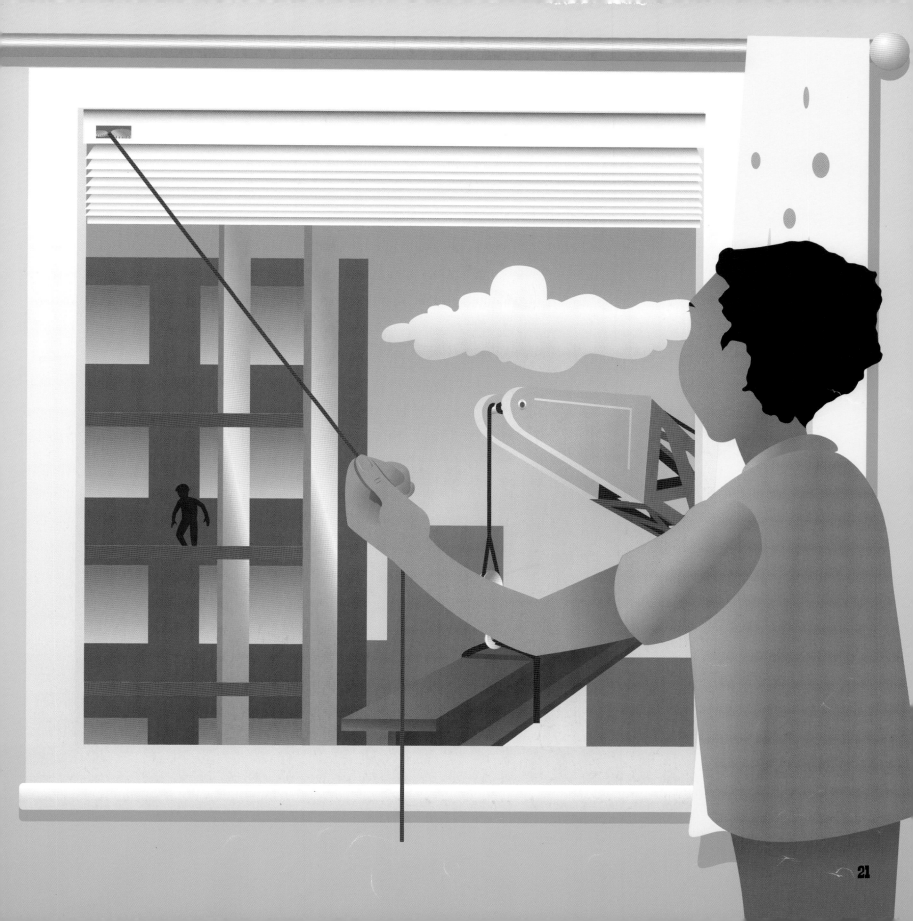

21

MESSAGE ON A PULLEY

Can you use a pulley to help you send messages across the room?

MATERIALS:

- 2 thread spools
- 40 feet (12 meters) of string
- 2 pencils
- paperclips
- message on a piece of paper

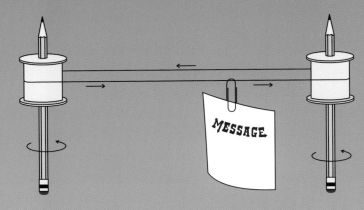

PROCEDURE:

1. Put the pencils through the thread spool centers. Tie the ends of the string together to make a loop. Have one person hold the end of one pencil, allowing the spool to turn freely. Have another person hold the other spool. Wrap the string around the spools to create a pulley system.

2. Write a message and attach it to the pulley with a paper clip. Have a third person pull the string to move the message.

Did your message travel across the room by pulley?

FOLLOW UP QUESTIONS:

1. What other things could you send using this pulley system?

2. Do you think it would be easier or harder to use bigger thread spools. Why?

FUN FACTS

The wheel on a pulley usually has a narrow channel along the middle. This channel is called a groove. The groove helps keep the rope from slipping off the pulley's wheel.

The pole of a flagpole is also called a staff or mast. Sometimes flags are used to honor people who have died. The flag is not raised to the very top. Instead, the flag is said to fly at half-mast.

If the cable of an elevator car is accidentally cut, the car will not fall. That only happens in movies. Small gears attached to the car will grab hold of the sides of the shaft. This will keep the car from dropping to the bottom of the elevator shaft.

GLOSSARY

axel—a pin or shaft on which a wheel or pair of wheels revolves

block and tackle—pulley blocks with associated rope or cable for hoisting or hauling

cable—a metal or wire rope

halyards—a rope or tackle for hoisting and lowering something, such as sails

pulley—a simple machine consisting of a wheel with a grooved rim and a rope or chain

TO LEARN MORE

AT THE LIBRARY

Douglas, Lloyd G. *What Is a Pulley?* New York:
Children's Press, 2002.

Fowler, Allan. *Simple Machines.* New York:
Children's Press, 2001.

Frost, Helen & Gail Saunders-Smith. *What Are
Pulleys.* Mankato, Minn.: Pebble Books, 2001.

Walker, Sally M & Roseann Feldmann. Minneapolis,
Minn.: *Pulleys.* Lerner, 2001.

ON THE WEB

FactHound offers a safe, fun way to find Internet sites
related to this book. All of the sites on FactHound have
been researched by our staff.

1. Visit *www.facthound.com*

2. Type in this special code for age-appropriate
   sites: *1404813055*

3. Click on the FETCH IT button. Your trusty
FactHound will fetch the best sites for you!

LOOK FOR ALL OF THE BOOKS IN THE AMAZING SCIENCE SERIES:

Air: Outside, Inside, and All Around	1-4048-0248-7	Pull, Lift, and Lower: A Book About Pulleys	1-4048-1305-5
Cut, Chop, and Stop: A Book About Wedges	1-4048-1307-1	Rocks: Hard, Soft, Smooth, and Rough	1-4048-0015-8
Dirt: The Scoop on Soil	1-4048-0012-3	Roll, Slope, and Slide: A Book About Ramps	1-4048-1304-7
Electricity: Bulbs, Batteries, and Sparks	1-4048-0245-2	Scoop, Seesaw, and Raise: A Book About Levers	1-4048-1303-9
Energy: Heat, Light, and Fuel	1-4048-0249-5	Sound: Loud, Soft, High, and Low	1-4048-0016-6
Light: Shadows, Mirrors, and Rainbows	1-4048-0013-1	Temperature: Heating Up and Cooling Down	1-4048-0247-9
Magnets: Pulling Together, Pushing Apart	1-4048-0014-X	Tires, Spokes, and Sprockets: A Book About Wheels	1-4048-1308-X
Matter: See It, Tough It, Taste It, Smell It	1-4048-0246-0	Twist, Dig, and Drill: A Book About Screws	1-4048-1306-3
Motion: Push and Pull, Fast and Slow	1-4048-0250-9	Water: Up, Down, and All Around	14048-0017-4a